EGYPT
MAGNIFIED

WIDE EYED EDITIONS

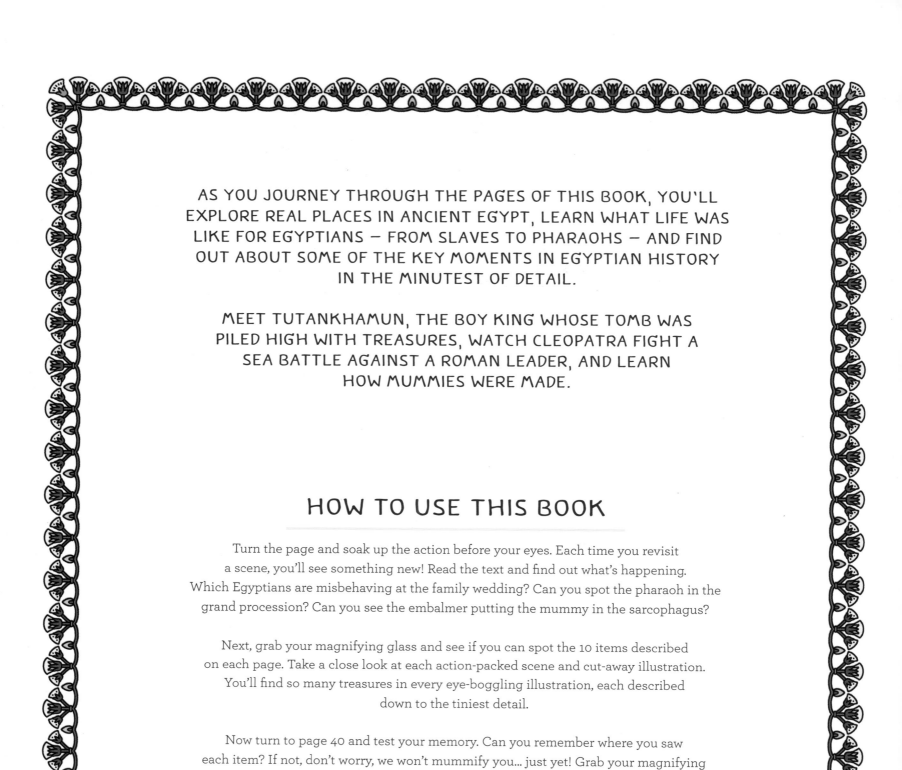

AS YOU JOURNEY THROUGH THE PAGES OF THIS BOOK, YOU'LL EXPLORE REAL PLACES IN ANCIENT EGYPT, LEARN WHAT LIFE WAS LIKE FOR EGYPTIANS – FROM SLAVES TO PHARAOHS – AND FIND OUT ABOUT SOME OF THE KEY MOMENTS IN EGYPTIAN HISTORY IN THE MINUTEST OF DETAIL.

MEET TUTANKHAMUN, THE BOY KING WHOSE TOMB WAS PILED HIGH WITH TREASURES, WATCH CLEOPATRA FIGHT A SEA BATTLE AGAINST A ROMAN LEADER, AND LEARN HOW MUMMIES WERE MADE.

HOW TO USE THIS BOOK

Turn the page and soak up the action before your eyes. Each time you revisit a scene, you'll see something new! Read the text and find out what's happening. Which Egyptians are misbehaving at the family wedding? Can you spot the pharaoh in the grand procession? Can you see the embalmer putting the mummy in the sarcophagus?

Next, grab your magnifying glass and see if you can spot the 10 items described on each page. Take a close look at each action-packed scene and cut-away illustration. You'll find so many treasures in every eye-boggling illustration, each described down to the tiniest detail.

Now turn to page 40 and test your memory. Can you remember where you saw each item? If not, don't worry, we won't mummify you... just yet! Grab your magnifying glass and go back for one more search-and-find adventure. You're bound to spot much more this time around. Lastly, learn how to write in hieroglyphics on page 38 and then turn to page 44 to study the timeline.

What are you waiting for? Discover the secrets of ancient Egypt before the tomb raiders beat you to it!

CONTENTS

THE NILE AND THE DESERT

Ancient Egypt was an enormous country in what is now North Africa. Much of the land was desert, but the River Nile flooded each year, so it was possible to grow crops and raise animals for food. Most Egyptians lived in towns near the river, which was more than 6,853 kilometres long. Their houses were built using bricks made of dried mud from the Nile. The desert protected the Egyptians from invaders – it was so hot and there was so little water that no one could have crossed it and survived.

10 THINGS TO SPOT

BOAT The oldest Nile boats were made of reeds called papyrus which grew along the riverbanks.

SHOES Egyptians made lots of other things out of papyrus, including paper, baskets, rope and even shoes.

SAIL The river current carried boats north, towards the sea, so a boat needed a sail to catch the wind in order to travel south.

NET Fishermen used nets, harpoons and hooks to catch fish. People went fishing for fun as well as to catch food.

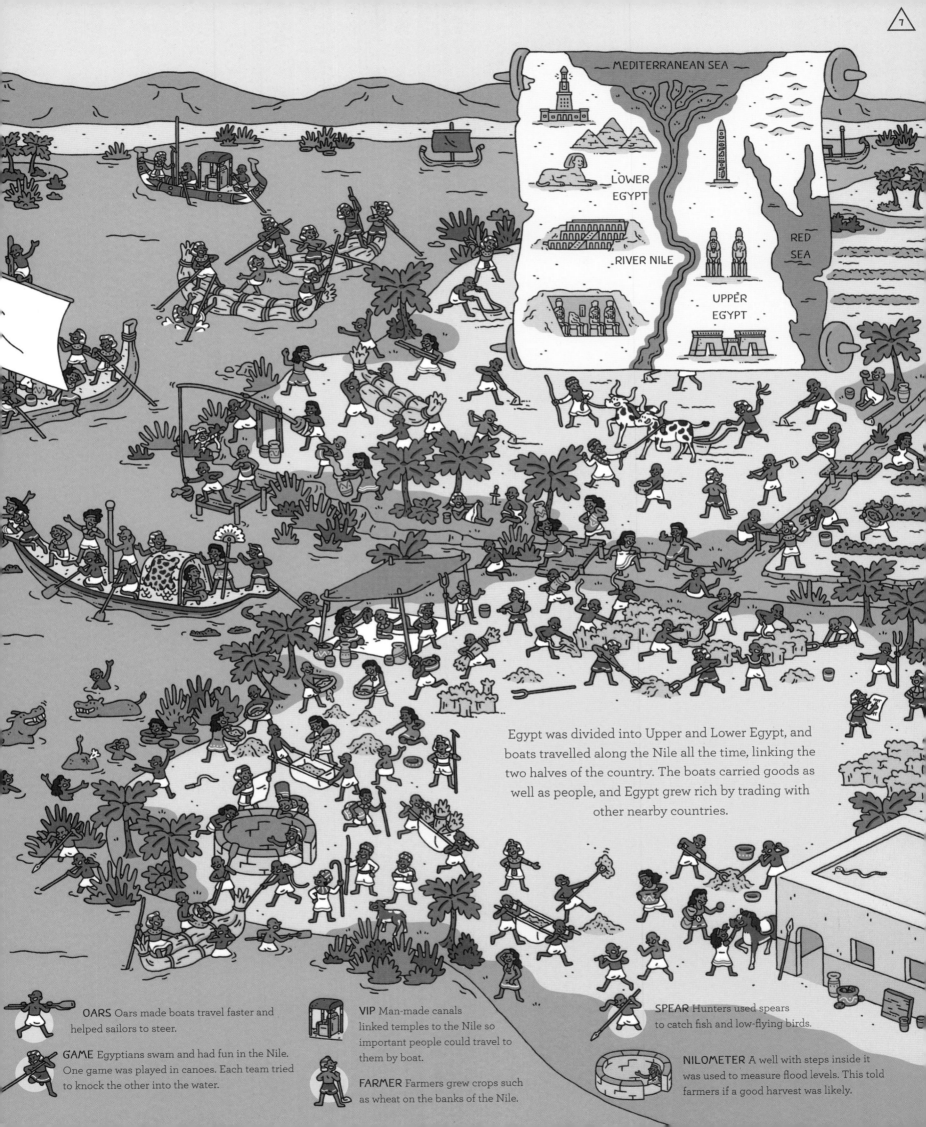

MEDITERRANEAN SEA

LOWER
EGYPT

RIVER NILE

UPPER
EGYPT

RED
SEA

Egypt was divided into Upper and Lower Egypt, and boats travelled along the Nile all the time, linking the two halves of the country. The boats carried goods as well as people, and Egypt grew rich by trading with other nearby countries.

OARS Oars made boats travel faster and helped sailors to steer.

GAME Egyptians swam and had fun in the Nile. One game was played in canoes. Each team tried to knock the other into the water.

VIP Man-made canals linked temples to the Nile so important people could travel to them by boat.

FARMER Farmers grew crops such as wheat on the banks of the Nile.

SPEAR Hunters used spears to catch fish and low-flying birds.

NILOMETER A well with steps inside it was used to measure flood levels. This told farmers if a good harvest was likely.

A FAMILY WEDDING

Men and women were considered equal in ancient Egypt.
Girls often got married when they were very young but they still
had the same legal rights as men. No one really knows what an
ancient Egyptian wedding ceremony involved. Some historians
think the bride's family simply carried her possessions from their
house to the groom's house, and the couple were considered
married. But ancient Egyptians loved feasts, music and dancing,
so they probably had a party to celebrate a wedding. At parties,
people wore their finest clothes and wigs and sat on the floor
to eat, chatting with friends and family, clapping along to the
musicians until the early hours of the morning.

10 THINGS TO SPOT

MAKE-UP Both men and women wore make-up.
They used eye shadow and eye liner made from minerals,
red ochre (a type of clay) to colour their lips and cheeks, and
dye from the henna plant to colour their hair and fingernails.

SENET Senet was a very popular board game.
It was a little bit like chess or checkers.

SPINNING TOP Children played with spinning tops,
dolls and toy animals. Archery (shooting with a bow and
arrow) and piggy-back-riding were very popular too.

LUTE Families hired musicians to play on special
occasions. They played harps, flutes and lutes,
which were a bit like modern guitars.

WIG Men and women shaved their heads to keep cool and to get rid of head lice. When they went out, they wore wigs. Children had shaved heads too, sometimes with a plait on one side.

WAX Party-goers often wore perfumed wax on top of their wigs to make themselves smell nice.

LOIN CLOTH Egyptian clothes were simple and light (young children didn't wear anything). Men often wore loin cloths – a single piece of cloth wrapped around the waist.

DANCER Groups of dancers entertained guests at dinner parties and banquets.

BEER Even children drank beer, because it was hard to find safe drinking water.

FISH Egyptians ate more fish than meat but duck, heron and pigeon were favourite dishes at banquets. They also liked sweet cakes made of dates and honey.

10 THINGS TO SPOT

SICKLE Egyptians harvested their crops using wooden sickles with blades made from a sharp stone called flint.

SHADUF Egyptians watered their crops by lifting water from the canals with a shaduf – a bucket on a rope attached to a large pole.

IRRIGATION DITCHES Man-made canals and ponds made it possible to water huge areas of dry land which could then be used for farming.

CHILD Reapers cut through the crops, and children and women followed behind, picking up anything that fell on the ground.

GROWING CROPS AND BUILDING HOUSES

Most Egyptians, young and old, worked on the land as farmers. Others were skilled craftsmen who built ordinary houses as well as great temples and pyramids that still exist today. If the river Nile hadn't flooded every year, the Egyptians wouldn't have been able to survive – the desert climate was too hot and dry. But the flood drenched the dry ground, leaving behind a rich soil, so they could grow crops and keep animals. Ancient Egyptians were among the first people to use a plough pulled by animals to loosen the soil after the flood, ready for seeds to be planted.

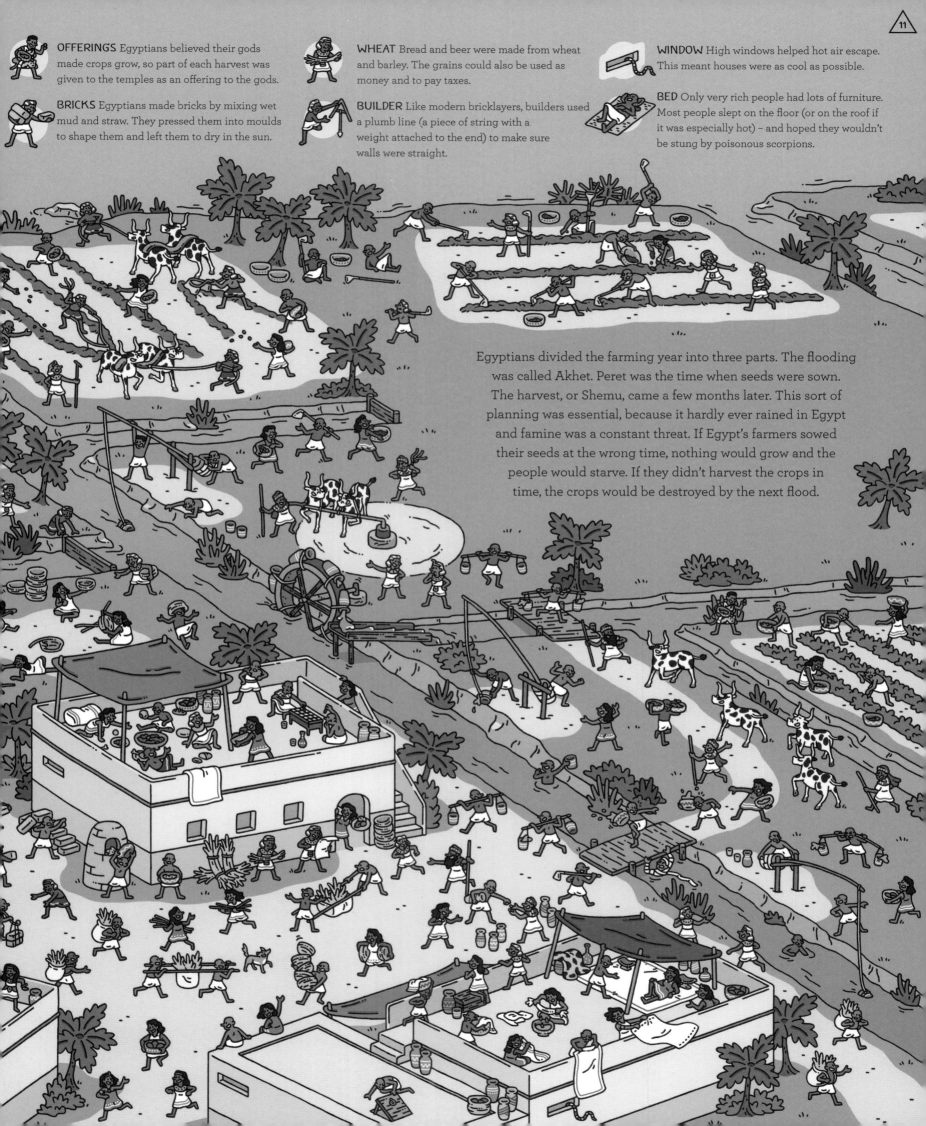

OFFERINGS Egyptians believed their gods made crops grow, so part of each harvest was given to the temples as an offering to the gods.

BRICKS Egyptians made bricks by mixing wet mud and straw. They pressed them into moulds to shape them and left them to dry in the sun.

WHEAT Bread and beer were made from wheat and barley. The grains could also be used as money and to pay taxes.

BUILDER Like modern bricklayers, builders used a plumb line (a piece of string with a weight attached to the end) to make sure walls were straight.

WINDOW High windows helped hot air escape. This meant houses were as cool as possible.

BED Only very rich people had lots of furniture. Most people slept on the floor (or on the roof if it was especially hot) – and hoped they wouldn't be stung by poisonous scorpions.

Egyptians divided the farming year into three parts. The flooding was called Akhet. Peret was the time when seeds were sown. The harvest, or Shemu, came a few months later. This sort of planning was essential, because it hardly ever rained in Egypt and famine was a constant threat. If Egypt's farmers sowed their seeds at the wrong time, nothing would grow and the people would starve. If they didn't harvest the crops in time, the crops would be destroyed by the next flood.

10 THINGS TO SPOT

STANDARD BEARER Officials walked in front of the pharaoh carrying standards or banners on long poles.

IMAGE OF RA One of the most important Egyptian gods was Ra, the sun god, who ruled over the sky, the earth and the underworld.

PRIEST Priests with shaved heads and leopard-skin capes sang chants in honour of the gods.

BUILDER As soon as a pharaoh was crowned, slaves began work on his tomb, as it would take years to complete.

THE PHARAOH

Egypt was ruled by a pharaoh – usually a king, but sometimes a queen. Egyptians believed the pharaoh was more than just a ruler – he was also the human incarnation of Horus, the god of the sky and kingship. When a pharaoh died, he joined the other gods in the afterlife, and a new pharaoh became Horus. The coronation of a new pharaoh involved many ceremonies and rich feasts. The celebrations could take up to a year. One of the most spectacular rituals was a procession called the Circumambulation of the White Walls. This took place in the capital, Memphis, which the Egyptians called Aneb-Hetch, or 'White Fortress'.

FEAST Ordinary Egyptians gathered to see the spectacle and to enjoy free food and wine, paid for by the pharaoh.

PHARAOH The pharaoh wore a double crown (Pschent) and carried a shepherd's crook (Heka) and a fly whip (Nekhakha).

PHARAOH'S SON Unlike ordinary Egyptians, pharaohs could have several wives. Ramses II had about 100 children.

HIGH PRIEST The chief priest wore pure white linen robes and splendid jewels.

SOKAR As part of the coronation, the pharaoh dragged a boat carrying a statue of Sokar, a god of the dead, to the river Nile. This marked the final passing of the old pharaoh.

SCULPTOR Sculptors carved new statues, showing the new pharaoh.

The procession involved hundreds of people, priests as well as powerful advisers to the pharaoh and his family, who followed the new ruler as he went around the walls. Normally the pharaoh would be carried by slaves or travel in a chariot, but by walking he reinforced his claim to the throne and demonstrated his power.

THE GREAT PYRAMID

One of the most famous of all the pharaohs is Khufu, who reigned from around 2609–2584 BC. Very little is known about Khufu's life, but he probably became pharaoh in his twenties, and as soon as he did, he ordered the construction of the pyramid that he would be buried in. Khufu's pyramid – the Great Pyramid of Giza – is the largest of all the Egyptian pyramids. It's made of more than 2.3 million stone blocks, each of which weigh between 2 and 15 tons, and took over 20 years to build. When Khufu's tomb was finished, it remained the tallest building on earth for nearly 4,000 years.

 THE BOSS The man in charge of building the Great Pyramid was called Hemiunu. He was a priest as well as being the pharaoh's vizier or highest official.

 WATER Builders probably used sledges to pull heavy stones across the sand. They wet the sand to make it easier to pull the sledge.

 BUILDER The Great Pyramid was built by around 100,000 paid workers. They lived in camps nearby.

 ENTRANCE The entrance was hidden more than 15 metres above the ground to prevent robbers stealing treasures from the tomb.

 KHUFU Khufu probably wanted his pyramid to be larger than his father's – and he got his wish!

 QUEEN'S PYRAMID Smaller pyramids were built nearby for Khufu's wives.

 PLANS The Great Pyramid is an amazing feat of engineering and the builders followed detailed plans.

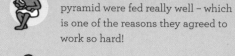 **LUNCH** The workers who built the pyramid were fed really well – which is one of the reasons they agreed to work so hard!

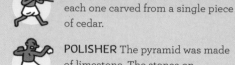 **OAR** Khufu's ship had twelve oars, each one carved from a single piece of cedar.

POLISHER The pyramid was made of limestone. The stones on the outside were polished to reflect the sun.

An entire ship was dismantled and buried in a carved stone pit next to the Great Pyramid. It is the oldest surviving ship in the world and may have been meant for the pharaoh to use in the afterlife.

GODS AND PRIESTS

Ancient Egyptians worshipped around 2,000 different gods, who they believed controlled the world and every aspect of their lives. The gods were often shown as having animal heads on human bodies. One of the most important was Horus, the god of the sky and of kingship, who was usually shown as a falcon or as a man with a falcon's head.

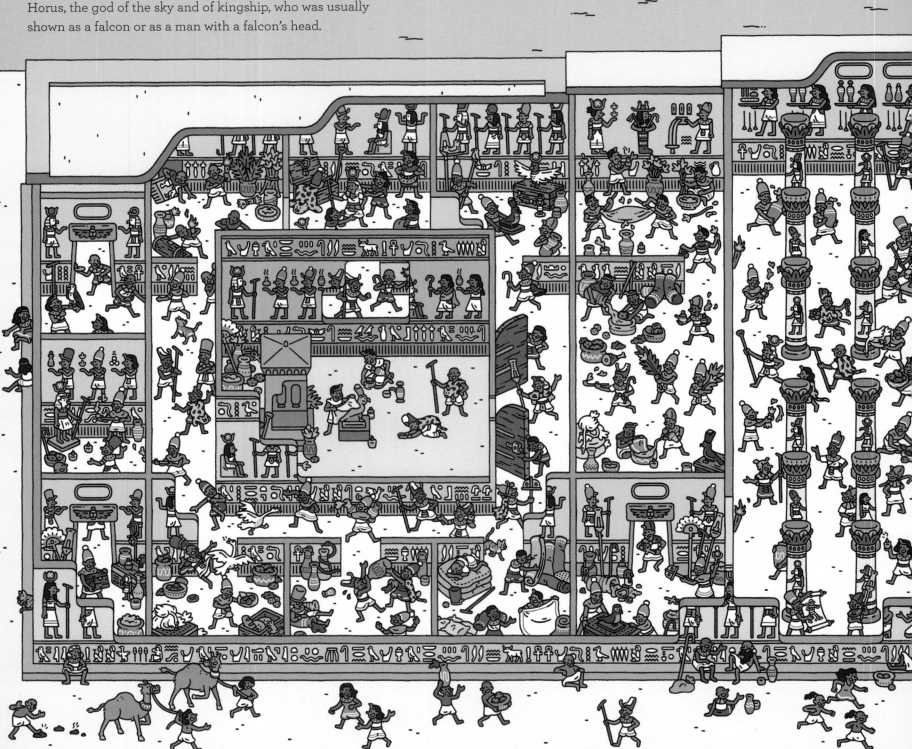

10 THINGS TO SPOT

 HORUS The statues of the gods were usually made of wood or stone and were sometimes covered with gold.

 LOCK The priests unlocked the temple each morning. At sunset, they sealed the doors. If the seal was broken in the morning, they could tell that someone had entered during the night.

 FALCON Sacred animals, including falcons, rams and bulls, lived in some of the temples. They were thought to represent different gods.

 AMULET Ancient Egyptians often wore amulets, or charms, showing symbols of the gods. They believed these brought them good luck and protected them from evil.

Every town and city had temples where the gods lived. Temple shrines contained statues of the gods but only priests were allowed inside to see them – ordinary people were locked out. (Door locks were an ancient Egyptian invention.) It was the pharaoh's job to look after the gods, but as he was busy ruling the country, priests did most of the hard work. They washed and dressed the statues every day, and 'fed' them food and water.

 CHIEF PRIEST The chief priest would lie down in front of a statue of a god to show respect.

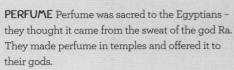 **PERFUME** Perfume was sacred to the Egyptians – they thought it came from the sweat of the god Ra. They made perfume in temples and offered it to their gods.

 OIL LAMP Temples were lit using oil lamps and torches made of rushes or dried plants.

 JEWELS The priests placed offerings of gold, precious jewels, food and drink in front of the statues.

 INCENSE Sweet-smelling incense was burned in the temple to please the gods.

 STATUE During religious festivals, statues of the gods were carried on priests' shoulders or placed in ceremonial boats so that the public could see them.

10 THINGS TO SPOT

ATEN Aten, the sun god, was represented as a circle with rays extending out of it. At the end of each ray was a hand.

CAT Cats were very important in ancient Egypt. The penalty for killing a cat was death.

TUTANKHAMUN Tutankhamun is the most famous of a pharaohs, even though he died when he was still a child. That's because his tomb, discovered in 1922, was the best preserved Egyptian tomb ever discovered.

BUST OF NEFERTITI Nefertiti, Akhenaten's wife, is one of the best-known queens of ancient Egypt. She may have ruled jointly with Akhenaten, or alone after his death.

AKHENATEN AND TUTANKHAMUN

Akhenaten ruled Egypt for seventeen years. He had six wives, including the beautiful Queen Nefertiti, and he is thought to have been the father of Tutankhamun, Egypt's famous boy king. Akhenaten's name was originally Amenhotep but he changed it to Akhenaten when he began to worship the sun, or Aten. Akhenaten tried to stop Egyptians worshipping all their other gods and he ordered a new capital city called Akhetaten to be built many miles away from Memphis, on the opposite bank of the River Nile. It had none of the temples or statues of the old religion, just places where Aten could be worshipped.

AKHENATEN A statue of Akhenaten shows him wearing a blue crown. This was worn by the pharaoh during ceremonies and when he was riding into battle.

STELA Fourteen stone slabs called stelae stood in a ring around the city. The carvings on them described how the city was built as a monument to Aten, the sun.

PALACE Akhenaten and Nefertiti lived in a large palace at the edge of the river Nile. The walls were decorated with painted friezes and blue tiles.

THIEF! The stones used to build the palaces and temples in Akhetaten were taken away and used to make other buildings.

LETTERS Hundreds of letters, written on clay tablets, were left behind in Akhetaten. These were mostly messages to the pharaoh from other important leaders.

BREAD AND BEER The workers who built the city lived in cramped conditions. Their meals were mostly bread and beer, so they weren't very healthy.

But the Egyptians loved their old traditions, and when Akhenaten and Nefertiti died, they went back to worshipping lots of different gods and goddesses, and Memphis became the capital of Egypt again. When Tutankhamun became pharaoh, he ordered his people to destroy temples honouring Aten. No one wanted to live in Akhetaten anymore. The city was mostly made of dried mud, so it quickly fell into ruins after everyone left.

HARD AT WORK

Life was very hard for slaves in ancient Egypt. Many were whipped and beaten as they worked outdoors in the burning heat of the sun, but others were luckier – they were given tasks to do in the towns and cities. Some were highly skilled men and women who looked after the temples and the houses and gardens of the rich. Others worked as musicians and dancers, or as scribes writing letters and official documents at a time when most people still couldn't read or write. Slaves didn't have the freedom to choose what jobs they did.

10 THINGS TO SPOT

GOLD Gold was very important to the ancient Egyptians. Because it doesn't decay, it was associated with everlasting life.

STRONG WORKER When the Egyptians defeated an army, they often took the soldiers into slavery. Soldiers were valued as slaves because they were usually fit and strong.

YOUNG SLAVE The children of slaves automatically became slaves as well. They were put to work as soon as they were old enough.

ROCK FALL Slaves working in mines had to watch out for falling rocks.

TORCH The only light in the mines came from burning torches which the slaves fixed to their foreheads.

HAMMER The slaves carried rock to the surface of the gold mine. They heated it on fires and smashed it with stone hammers to extract the metal.

MILL The smashed rock and metal was ground in mills to turn it into a powder. Two or three people turned each mill. It was hard work, and they weren't allowed to rest.

WATER The powder was spread on sloping tables. Water flowed over the powder to wash away the earth and leave the heavier gold behind.

BOSS Slaves who worked in gold mines were often treated cruelly by their bosses.

SPONGE Workers rubbed the gold dust with sponges to make it shine.

Slaves who were sent to one of the pharaoh's mines had to work in the desert heat and faced terrible dangers such as rock falls and suffocation. Digging for gemstones and precious metals such as gold, silver and copper was one of the worst jobs for a slave.

10 THINGS TO SPOT

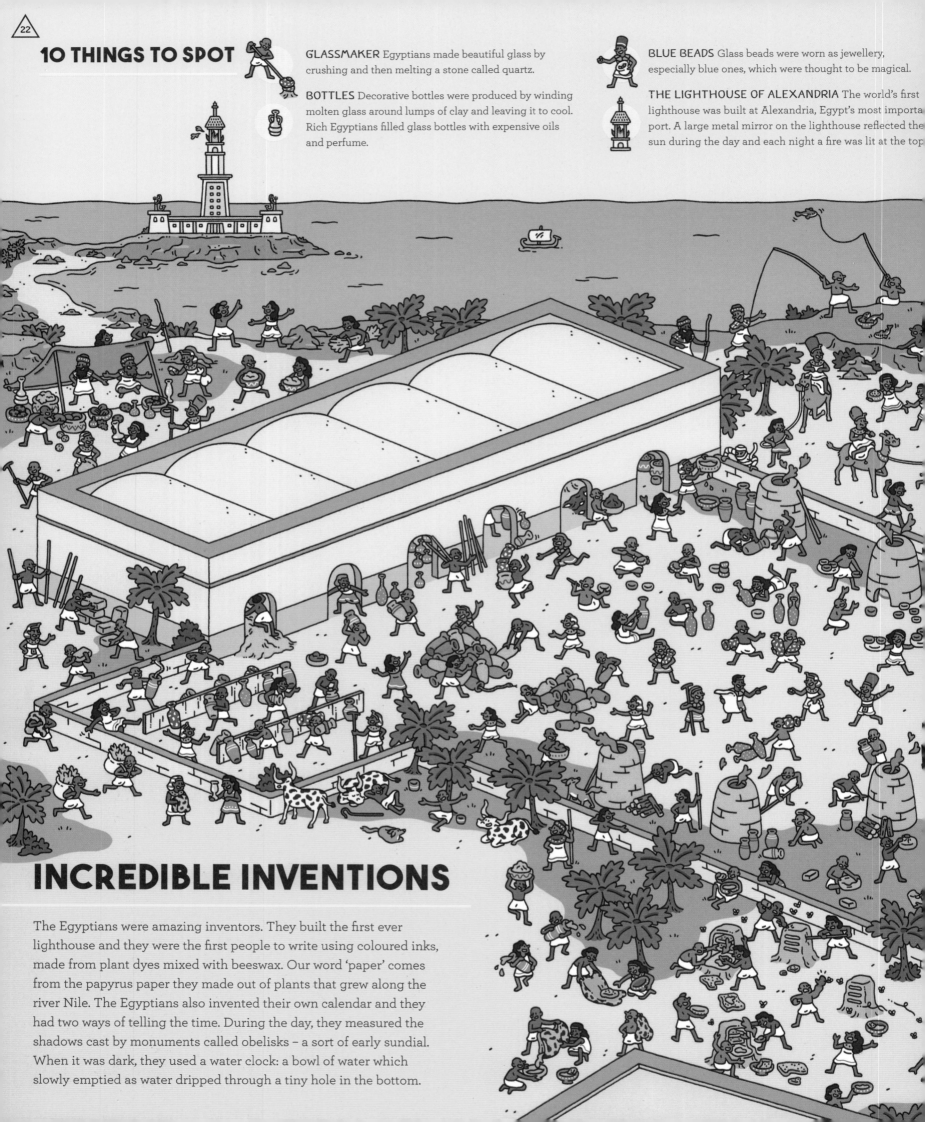

GLASSMAKER Egyptians made beautiful glass by crushing and then melting a stone called quartz.

BOTTLES Decorative bottles were produced by winding molten glass around lumps of clay and leaving it to cool. Rich Egyptians filled glass bottles with expensive oils and perfume.

BLUE BEADS Glass beads were worn as jewellery, especially blue ones, which were thought to be magical.

THE LIGHTHOUSE OF ALEXANDRIA The world's first lighthouse was built at Alexandria, Egypt's most importa... port. A large metal mirror on the lighthouse reflected the sun during the day and each night a fire was lit at the top.

INCREDIBLE INVENTIONS

The Egyptians were amazing inventors. They built the first ever lighthouse and they were the first people to write using coloured inks, made from plant dyes mixed with beeswax. Our word 'paper' comes from the papyrus paper they made out of plants that grew along the river Nile. The Egyptians also invented their own calendar and they had two ways of telling the time. During the day, they measured the shadows cast by monuments called obelisks – a sort of early sundial. When it was dark, they used a water clock: a bowl of water which slowly emptied as water dripped through a tiny hole in the bottom.

PAPYRUS Papyrus was a kind of thick paper, made from reeds.

MINERALS Glassmakers added minerals to quartz to colour the glass. These included iron (yellow), cobalt (blue), copper (blue-green), and manganese (purple).

OBELISK Obelisks are tall pillars with pyramid-shaped points at the top. By measuring where an obelisk's shadow fell, Egyptians could work out what time it was.

CALENDAR In the Egyptian calendar, each month had thirty days, with five extra days added at the end of the year to make a total of 365.

INGOTS Small blocks of coloured glass called ingots were traded for goods with merchants from other countries. These were less likely to break on the journey than vases or bottles.

TRITON The statues at each corner of the Lighthouse of Alexandria represented a sea god called Triton.

They made toothpaste by grinding up salt, mint, petals and pepper, and made breath-freshening pills by boiling up tree resins called frankincense and myrrh with spiced honey.

IMHOTEP

The first Egyptian pyramid is known as the Djoser pyramid. It was built for the pharaoh Djoser by one of his most trusted advisers, Imhotep. Imhotep was a priest, but he was also a brilliant mathematician and a scientist (though the ancient Egyptians didn't have words for 'science' and 'scientist'). His intelligence and skill helped him rise from humble beginnings to become a very powerful man in Egyptian society. After his death, he was worshipped as the god of wisdom.

10 THINGS TO SPOT

STONE BLOCK Imhotep was the first person to build using stone blocks rather than mud. The stepped sides of the Djoser pyramid may have been a stairway for the pharaoh to climb towards the sun-god, Ra.

OPEN UP! Imhotep included several false doors in the high wall around the pyramid to trick grave robbers.

MUMMIFIED DOG Animals were sometimes mummified and buried as offerings to the gods.

COLUMN An entrance colonnade was formed by rows of stone columns. These were carved to look like bundles of plant stalks.

IMHOTEP Imhotep is often pictured wearing a blue skullcap, or calotte, to suggest he was the son of Ptah, the god of craftsmen and architects.

PHARAOH DJOSER When Djoser died, he was buried beneath the pyramid in the middle of a maze of tunnels stretching more than five kilometres.

MATHEMATICIAN Egyptian mathematicians like Imhotep probably used the stars to position the pyramids so that the four sides faced north, south, east and west.

ROPE Egyptian builders and architects used ropes to measure distances.

DOCTOR Egyptian doctors were able to perform surgery, set broken bones and heal wounds.

HERBAL REMEDY Egyptian doctors used herbal remedies to treat their patients. Some were effective, such as honey, which is a powerful antiseptic. Some weren't – animal dung was prescribed to treat some illnesses, which might have made patients sicker.

Imhotep was the first person to explain that illness is a natural thing and not a punishment from the gods. He wrote instructions about how to operate on patients, and how to use herbs as remedies. Many of his cures wouldn't have worked, but they were very advanced for the time.

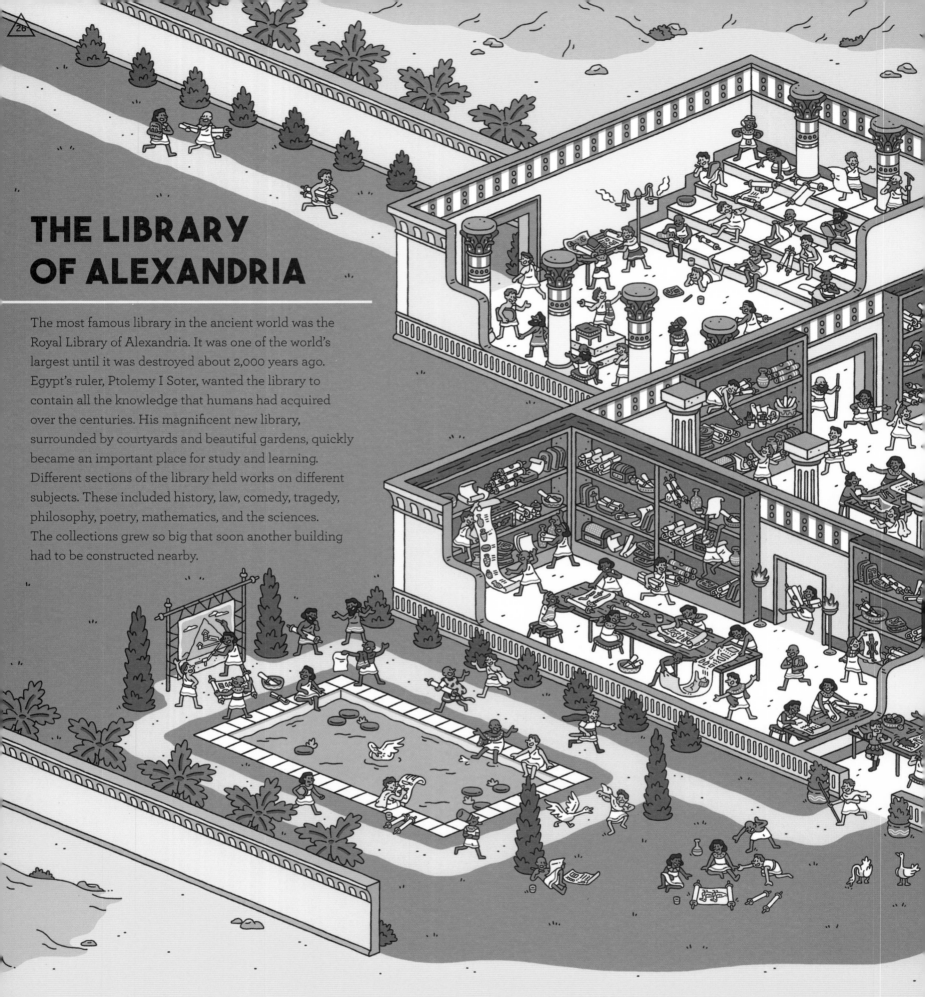

THE LIBRARY OF ALEXANDRIA

The most famous library in the ancient world was the Royal Library of Alexandria. It was one of the world's largest until it was destroyed about 2,000 years ago. Egypt's ruler, Ptolemy I Soter, wanted the library to contain all the knowledge that humans had acquired over the centuries. His magnificent new library, surrounded by courtyards and beautiful gardens, quickly became an important place for study and learning. Different sections of the library held works on different subjects. These included history, law, comedy, tragedy, philosophy, poetry, mathematics, and the sciences. The collections grew so big that soon another building had to be constructed nearby.

10 THINGS TO SPOT

SCROLL Books hadn't been invented yet, so the information in the library was stored on papyrus scrolls.

MERCHANT Merchants and travellers brought documents to the library from places such as Greece and the Roman Empire.

READER Scrolls had to be unrolled before they could be read. One piece of work might fill several scrolls.

HEAD LIBRARIAN The head librarian was the most important person in the library. He was usually Greek rather than Egyptian – Egypt was ruled by Greek leaders at the time.

Disaster struck about 240 years after Ptolemy's death. During a war with Rome, the main library caught fire and burned down. Almost everything inside was destroyed. No one knows whether the fire was started deliberately or by accident.

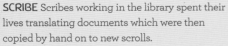

SCRIBE Scribes working in the library spent their lives translating documents which were then copied by hand on to new scrolls.

SCHOLAR Scholars came to the library to study the scrolls. They worked at tables in the library rather than taking the scrolls away.

LECTURER The library also included rooms and lecture halls where visitors could hear great thinkers talking about their work.

BREAK TIME Writers and philosophers often walked in the gardens where they could discuss important ideas.

LUNCH There was a dining room in the library where people could eat together and talk.

COLLECTOR Sometimes the scribes made special copies of the rarest scrolls. These were sold to rich collectors for huge sums of money which helped to pay for the library.

DEATH AND MUMMIES

The first Egyptian mummies were made by accident. For centuries, Egyptians buried their dead in shallow pits in the hot desert sand. The sand dried the bodies out quickly, preserving them for hundreds, even thousands of years. As people grew richer, they began placing the dead in baskets or wooden coffins. This offered protection from wild animals, but a body was more likely to decay if it was not in contact with the sand. The Egyptians thought the dead needed their bodies for the afterlife, so they came up with a way of preserving them, called mummification. Mummification was carried out by priests. They removed the body's internal organs, and covered the corpse with salt.

10 THINGS TO SPOT

 EMBALMER Priests who preserved bodies were called embalmers. They washed each body before removing the internal organs.

 CANOPIC JAR Internal organs were stored in containers called canopic jars. These were decorated with the heads of animal gods.

 HOOK Long metal hooks were used to pull the brain out through the nostrils. The heart was usually left in the mummy because Egyptians thought it was the centre of a person's memory and intelligence.

 ROPE If the embalmers lost or damaged the intestines one of the jars was filled with a length of rope.

The body was left covered in salt for 40 days, to dry out. The priests then poured perfumed oils, beeswax and sticky resins onto the body. Finally, they wrapped it in strips of linen which became stiff and hard as the resin dried.

SALT The salt used to preserve the body was called natron. The Egyptians collected it from dry lake beds in the desert.

ANUBIS The Egyptians worshipped a god of mummification called Anubis. He had a human body and a jackal's head.

SAWDUST The dried body was sometimes stuffed with sawdust or cloth.

SYMBOLS When the bandage-like wrapping on a mummy was dry, it was painted with magical symbols and decorations. These were believed to protect the mummy from evil.

SARCOPHAGUS Before being buried, the decorated mummy was placed in a large stone box called a sarcophagus.

CHAIR Furniture, games, jewellery, bowls and even food were buried with the mummy, so that the dead person could to use them in the afterlife. These were called grave goods.

10 THINGS TO SPOT

WALL PAINTING Deep in the heart of the pyramid was the pharaoh's burial chamber. It was richly decorated with carvings and paintings.

PHARAOH'S SARCOPHAGUS The pharaoh's mummified body was placed inside a huge sarcophagus with a heavy stone lid to keep it safe.

RUBBLE Inside the pyramid were hundreds of metres of steep, narrow passages. Sometimes the passages were blocked by large stones or rubble.

DEAD END Some passages didn't lead anywhere. These dummies or dead-ends were probably meant to trick the robbers and to lead them away from the pharaoh's chamber.

TOMB RAIDERS!

The ancient Egyptians are probably most famous for their pyramids – the vast tombs built for pharaohs and their wives. More than a hundred pyramids were built over a period of about 2,000 years, and they are still some of the largest buildings ever constructed. Deep inside them, Egyptians tried all sorts of tricks to stop anyone stealing the gold and other treasures which were buried with the dead. Robbing a grave was one of the most serious crimes in Egypt. Anyone caught doing it was tortured and killed. Egyptians believed that after the thieves were dead they would be punished again by the gods they had offended. Incredibly, even this wasn't enough to prevent robbers raiding the tombs.

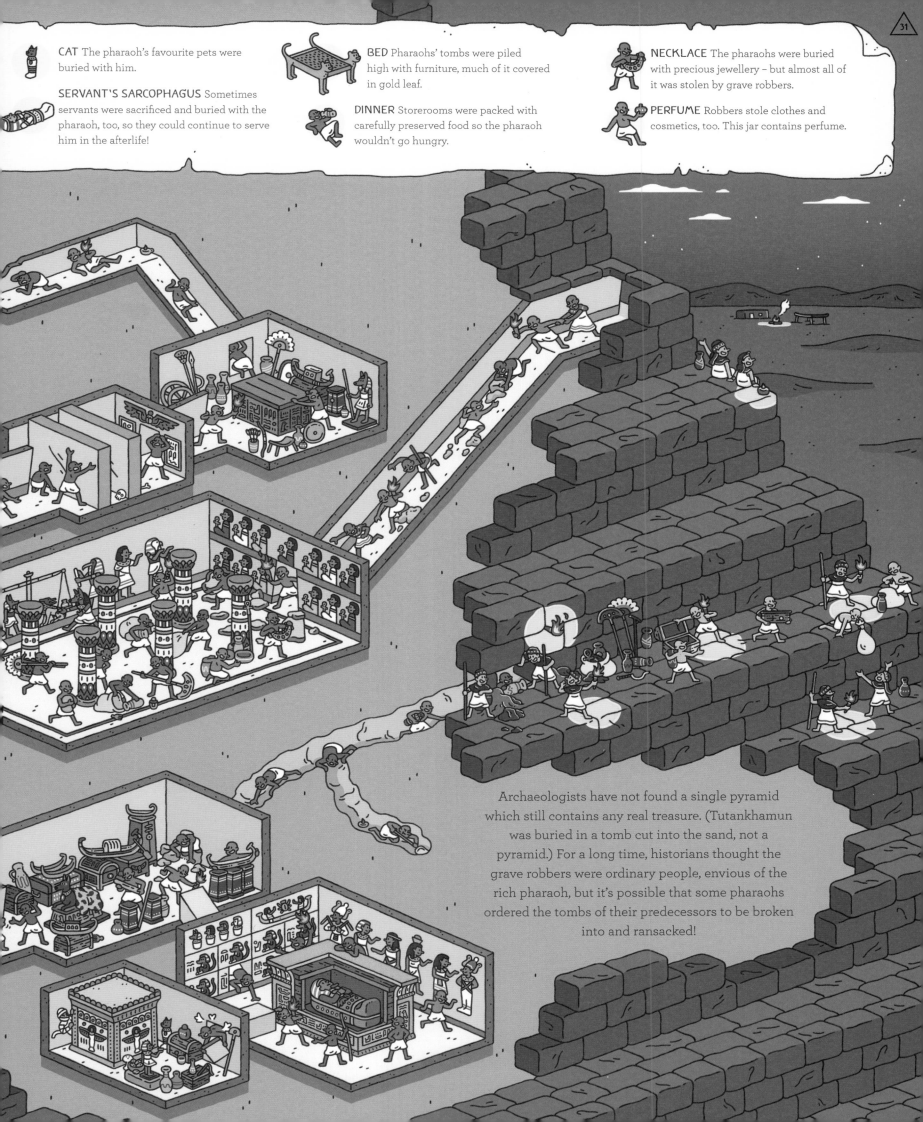

CAT The pharaoh's favourite pets were buried with him.

SERVANT'S SARCOPHAGUS Sometimes servants were sacrificed and buried with the pharaoh, too, so they could continue to serve him in the afterlife!

BED Pharaohs' tombs were piled high with furniture, much of it covered in gold leaf.

DINNER Storerooms were packed with carefully preserved food so the pharaoh wouldn't go hungry.

NECKLACE The pharaohs were buried with precious jewellery – but almost all of it was stolen by grave robbers.

PERFUME Robbers stole clothes and cosmetics, too. This jar contains perfume.

Archaeologists have not found a single pyramid which still contains any real treasure. (Tutankhamun was buried in a tomb cut into the sand, not a pyramid.) For a long time, historians thought the grave robbers were ordinary people, envious of the rich pharaoh, but it's possible that some pharaohs ordered the tombs of their predecessors to be broken into and ransacked!

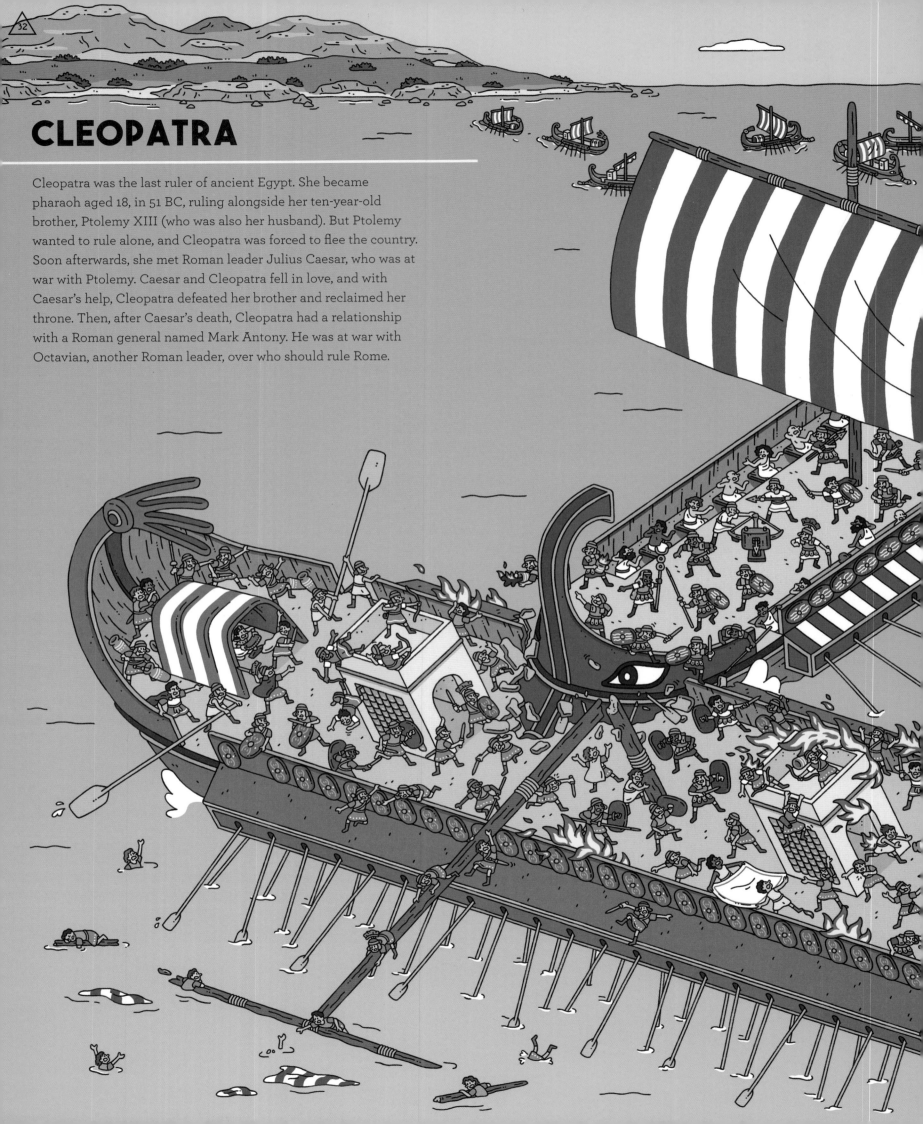

CLEOPATRA

Cleopatra was the last ruler of ancient Egypt. She became pharaoh aged 18, in 51 BC, ruling alongside her ten-year-old brother, Ptolemy XIII (who was also her husband). But Ptolemy wanted to rule alone, and Cleopatra was forced to flee the country. Soon afterwards, she met Roman leader Julius Caesar, who was at war with Ptolemy. Caesar and Cleopatra fell in love, and with Caesar's help, Cleopatra defeated her brother and reclaimed her throne. Then, after Caesar's death, Cleopatra had a relationship with a Roman general named Mark Antony. He was at war with Octavian, another Roman leader, over who should rule Rome.

10 THINGS TO SPOT

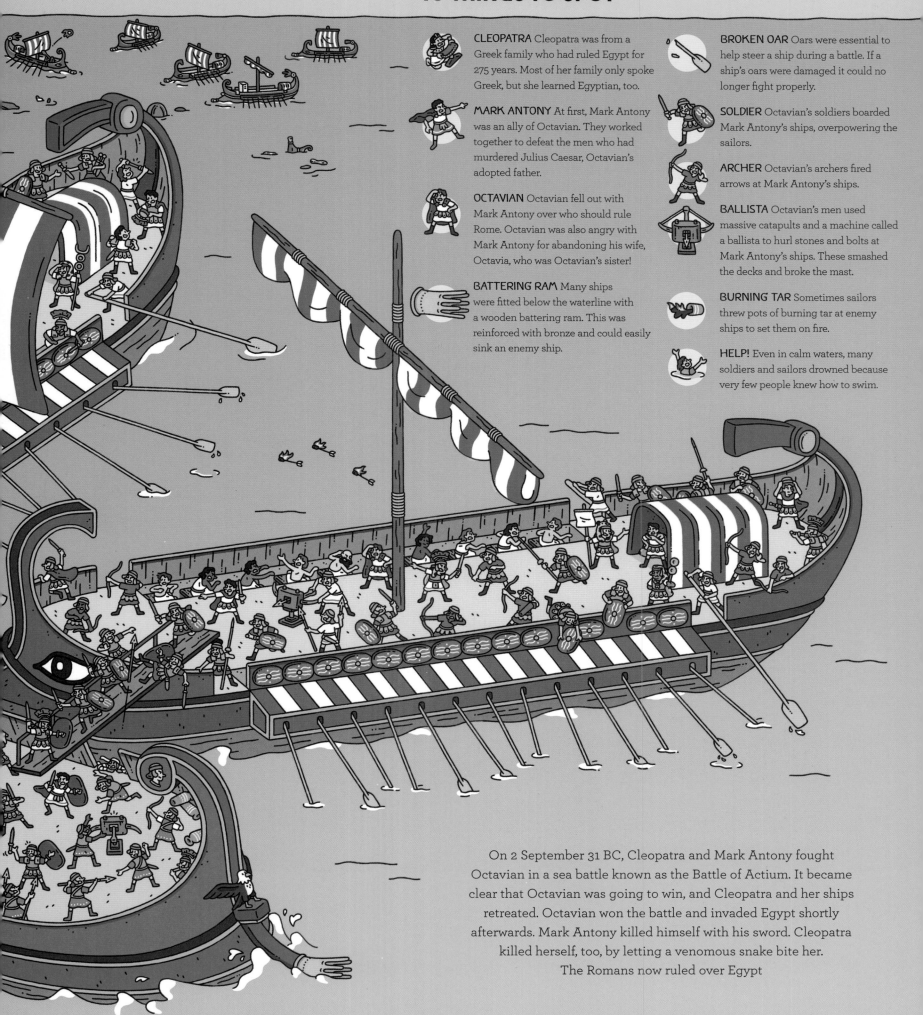

CLEOPATRA Cleopatra was from a Greek family who had ruled Egypt for 275 years. Most of her family only spoke Greek, but she learned Egyptian, too.

MARK ANTONY At first, Mark Antony was an ally of Octavian. They worked together to defeat the men who had murdered Julius Caesar, Octavian's adopted father.

OCTAVIAN Octavian fell out with Mark Antony over who should rule Rome. Octavian was also angry with Mark Antony for abandoning his wife, Octavia, who was Octavian's sister!

BATTERING RAM Many ships were fitted below the waterline with a wooden battering ram. This was reinforced with bronze and could easily sink an enemy ship.

BROKEN OAR Oars were essential to help steer a ship during a battle. If a ship's oars were damaged it could no longer fight properly.

SOLDIER Octavian's soldiers boarded Mark Antony's ships, overpowering the sailors.

ARCHER Octavian's archers fired arrows at Mark Antony's ships.

BALLISTA Octavian's men used massive catapults and a machine called a ballista to hurl stones and bolts at Mark Antony's ships. These smashed the decks and broke the mast.

BURNING TAR Sometimes sailors threw pots of burning tar at enemy ships to set them on fire.

HELP! Even in calm waters, many soldiers and sailors drowned because very few people knew how to swim.

On 2 September 31 BC, Cleopatra and Mark Antony fought Octavian in a sea battle known as the Battle of Actium. It became clear that Octavian was going to win, and Cleopatra and her ships retreated. Octavian won the battle and invaded Egypt shortly afterwards. Mark Antony killed himself with his sword. Cleopatra killed herself, too, by letting a venomous snake bite her. The Romans now ruled over Egypt

THE RIDDLE OF THE SPHINX

There is still so much we don't understand about ancient Egypt. The Great Sphinx of Giza is one of the most famous monuments in the world but no one knows who made it, when it was made or what it's for. Archaeologists have always called it the Sphinx, after the ancient Greek name for a creature with the head of a human and the body of a lion.

The Sphinx is 73 metres long and over 20 metres tall – as tall as a seven-storey building. It's one of the largest stone carvings anywhere in the world. Most historians think the face represents the pharaoh Khafre and that it was built to protect his pyramid. Over thousands of years, the limestone has been worn away by countless sandstorms. For centuries, it was almost buried by sand, and several hundred years ago the nose fell off and was lost.

HERE ARE SOME FAMOUS EGYPTIANS THAT WE *DO* KNOW ABOUT!

AMENHOTEP I
1526–1506 BC

As pharaoh, Amenhotep built so many temples and monuments that grateful workmen began to worship him as a god.

CLEOPATRA
51–30 BC

Cleopatra was the last pharaoh of Egypt. She was extremely intelligent and a brilliant politician.

HATSHEPSUT
1479–1458 BC

Hatshepsut was the second female pharaoh. She built great temples and extended trade routes and she's remembered as one of the most successful pharaohs.

KHAFRE
2558–2532 BC

The pharaoh with the second largest pyramid. Some historians think that his face was used as the model for the Sphinx's face.

WATCH OUT! The Sphinx was carved out of a single piece of limestone. This rock is soft, so parts of it have been worn away by flood water, wind and rain.

SAND For centuries, parts of the Sphinx were buried in sand that was blown over the statue by the wind.

SECRET TUNNEL There are three passages into or under the Sphinx. One was excavated during the 19th century but the others haven't been explored.

HOLES Small holes in the Sphinx's body may have been made to hold up the scaffolding used by the people who carved the statue.

RESTORER About thirty years ago, the Sphinx's left shoulder began to crumble. Scientists are still looking for a way to save the Sphinx for future generations.

TAIL The Sphinx has a tail which wraps around one of its back paws.

ALTAR The remains of a granite altar have been found between the Sphinx's front paws.

NOSE The Sphinx's nose is missing. It was probably knocked off deliberately hundreds of years ago, but no one knows why.

CANNON DAMAGE Other damage to the face may have been caused by a cannon fired by French soldiers during a war at the end of the 18th century.

SCRAP OF PAINT Traces of red and blue paint have been found on the Sphinx's face. Some experts believe it may once have been painted in bright colours.

AKHENATEN
1352–1334 BC
This powerful pharaoh built a new city called Akhetaten. He tried to replace all the Egyptian gods with just one: Aten.

KHUFU
2589–2566 BC
Also known as Cheops, Khufu is the only pharaoh to have an even larger pyramid than Khafre.

NEFERTITI
1370–1330 BC
Nefertiti was the wife of Akhenaten and probably ruled as pharaoh after his death. She worshipped just one god, Aten.

RAMSES II
1279–1213 BC
Ramses reigned for 67 years and outlived all 12 of his sons. He put his name on monuments built by previous pharaohs and declared himself a god.

TUTANKHAMUN
1336–1327 BC
Tutankhamun was a young pharaoh who didn't rule for long. But he is very famous, because when his tomb was discovered in 1922 it was still full of amazing treasures.

10 THINGS TO SPOT

HOWARD CARTER Archaeologist Howard Carter had been searching for Tutankhamun's tomb for years before he finally found it on 4 November 1922.

LORD CARNARVON Wealthy aristocrat Lord Carnarvon took up archaeology as a hobby and provided Howard Carter with the money he needed to hunt for ancient Egyptian treasures.

STEPS Tutankhamun was buried underground, not in a pyramid. Howard Carter discovered 16 steps that led down into the tomb.

PAINTED BOX The rooms were crammed with furniture, jewels and gold. One of the greatest treasures was a painted box decorated with a picture of Tutankhamun riding his chariot.

TUTANKHAMUN'S TOMB

The first ancient Egyptians lived 5,000 years ago, so it's amazing that we know anything about them at all. We're discovering new things all the time thanks to archaeology. Archaeologists study history by excavating (digging up) historical sites and examining the things that are found. Many sites in Egypt have been excavated but there are probably hundreds more waiting to be discovered. The most spectacular discovery so far is Tutankhamen's tomb in the Valley of the Kings. Many royal tombs were found before his, but the others had been looted by robbers long before the archaeologists arrived.

GLOVES The tomb contained everything the pharaoh would need in the afterlife, including clothes and clean underwear. It took ten years to catalogue the 5,398 different items.

SHRINE This golden shrine contains Tutankhamun's internal organs.

DAGGER One of the strangest finds was a dagger with a blade made of a carved meteorite from outer space. To the Egyptians this might have been even more valuable than gold.

TRUMPETS Two trumpets found in the tomb are the oldest ever discovered. There's a recording of one of them being played, but they won't be played again as they are extremely fragile.

COFFIN Tutankhamun's mummy was protected by three coffins. Two were made of wood but the inner one was solid gold. This had gone black, probably from liquid poured over it by priests at his funeral.

STATUE This lifesize statue of the king is known as a guardian of the Ka, or spirit. It guarded the entrance to the burial chamber.

HIEROGLYPHICS

Ancient Egyptians used an alphabet of symbols called hieroglyphics. For centuries, no one knew how to read them – they were like a secret code. But in 1799, soldiers building a fortress in Egypt uncovered a large black rock called the Rosetta Stone. The same text was carved into the surface of the stone in three different forms of writing: Egyptian hieroglyphics, ancient Greek and Demotic (another kind of writing from Egypt). After years of study, historians used the Greek to work out what the hieroglyphics meant. Here is the alphabet in hieroglyphics. You can use it to write messages that no one else can read. The words in brackets next to the letters show what the symbols represent.

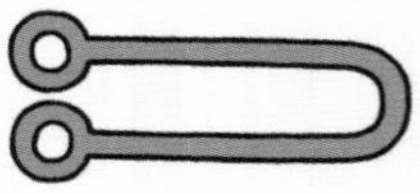

CH (ROPE)

KH (SIEVE)

SH (BASIN)

MAN

WOMAN

ANKH

A (VULTURE)

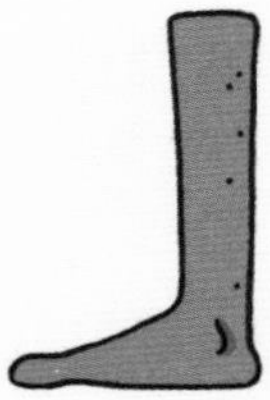

B (LEG)

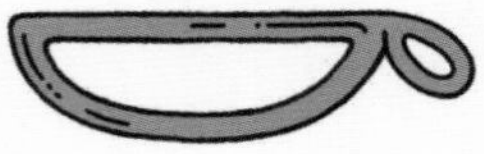

C (CUP)

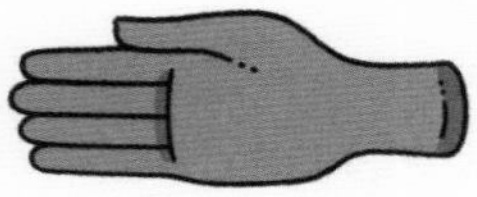

D (HAND)

E (FEATHER)

F (VIPER)

G (POT)

H (WICK)

I (FEATHERS)

J (COBRA)

K (CUP)

L (LION)

M (OWL)

N (WATER)

O (CHICK)

P (STOOL)

Q (HILL)

R (MOUTH)

S (CLOTH)

T (LOAF)

U (CHICK)

V (VIPER)

W (CHICK)

X (CLOTH)

Y (FEATHERS)

Z (BOLT)

CAN YOU FIND?

Take a look at the items below and see if you can remember which scene in the book they appear in. If you haven't seen them before, now's your chance to hunt them down by turning back to each action-packed scene for a second look. Don't forget to use your magnifying glass to study the finer detail in each spread. Plus there's a mummy hidden on every spread – can you find them all?

FIRE!

FARTING HIPPO

TAKING A NAP

MAN ON A STATUE

SKULL

HELP!

SAND ANGEL

BROKEN STATUE

TRAPPED!

COMFORTABLE BED

BUCKET HEAD

ALIEN STONE SLAB

STUNG BY BEES

HAPPY CAT

LENDING A HAND

CROCODILE

BUILDING BLOCKS

STARGAZING

TOY BIRD

PILE OF PAPYRUS

FLYING UNDERWEAR

BOW AND ARROW

SLEEPING MAN

MUSCLEY MAN

COLLECTING HONEY

A DRONE

PHOTOGRAPHER

MAN BEING SICK

SCORPION

CLIMBING THE SHELVES

SHAVING

FRIENDLY FALCON

ANGRY SWAN

EXIT!

CHILLING OUT

SMELLY FEET

VERY IMPORTANT CAT

FALLING SOLDIER

DINOSAUR SKULL

FLOATING

POOING HORSE

TOURISTS

SAND SLIDE

HAIRDRESSER

BASKET OF BONES

STEPPING IN POO

BASKET HAT

OUCH!

SHOULDER RIDE

CHEERS!

INJURED FOOT

TOPPLING JARS

GOAT ATTACK

HIDING

CARVED HEAD

STUCK IN A BUSH

CATCH OF THE DAY

ANSWERS

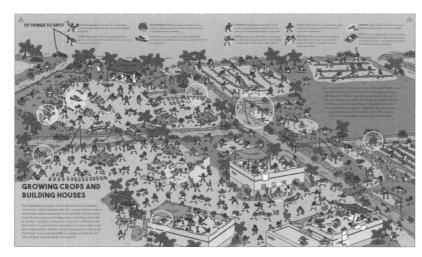

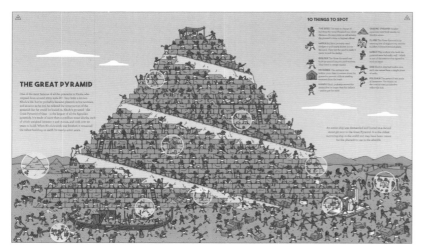

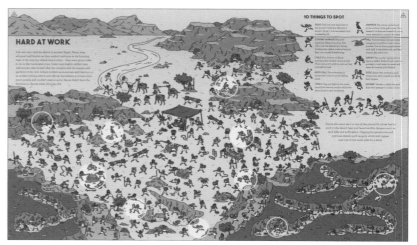

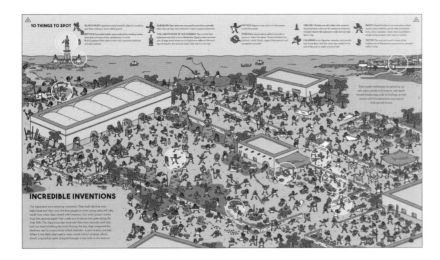

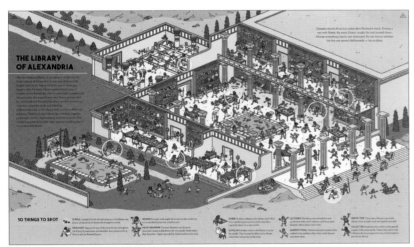

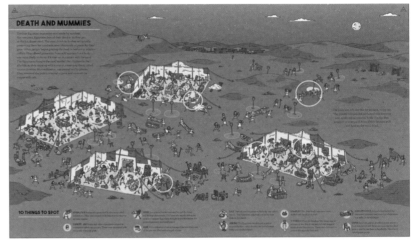

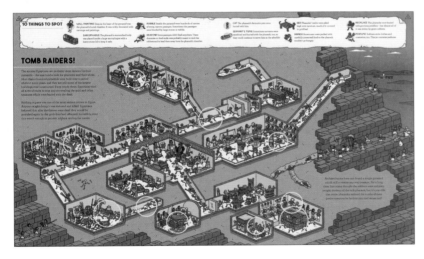

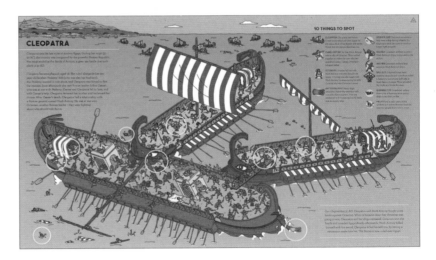

TIMELINE

6000 BC
- Tribes move into the Nile Valley.
- Clay from the river Nile is used to make pottery.

→ **5000 BC**
- Settlers begin to grow crops such as wheat and barley on the fertile land.

2950 BC–2575 BC
- Imhotep, a high priest, builds Pharaoh Djoser's pyramid.
- Memphis is established as the capital of Egypt.
- People began writing on papyrus.

← **3100 BC–2950 BC**
- Egyptian civilization is established by King Narmer.
- The north and south of Egypt are united.
- The first hieroglyphic writing is developed.
- Houses are made of dried mud from the Nile.

← **4500 BC**
- Boats with sails are used on the Nile for the first time. These are soon the main form of transport in the region.

2575 BC–2150 BC
- The great pyramids and the Sphinx are built at Giza.
- Egyptians begin to mummify dead bodies.

→ **2025 BC–1700 BC**
- The Book of the Dead – a book of spells intended to help a dead person pass through the Afterlife – is created.

→ **2000 BC**
- Horse-drawn chariots are used for the first time.

715 BC–332 BC
- Egypt is conquered by Persian king Cambyses II, and then again by Alexander the Great from Greece.

← **1520BC–1075 BC**
- Akhenaten and Nefertiti rule and attempt to replace all other gods with Aten.
- Royal burials move to the Valley of the Kings.
- Tutankhamen reigns briefly.
- Hatshepsut reigns as the first female Pharaoh.

← **1975BC–1640 BC**
- Thebes replaces Memphis as the capital of Egypt.

196 BC
- The Rosetta Stone is carved.

 51–30 BC
- Cleopatra VII reigns as pharaoh.
- She has a son with the Roman emperor, Julius Caesar, and later with Mark Antony, one of his generals.

 30 BC
- The Romans conquer Egypt and it becomes a province of the Roman Empire.

1922
- Archaeologists make an amazing discovery: Tutankhamun's tomb, full of gold and treasures.

 969 AD
- Armies from the Fatimid caliphate in North Africa take over Egypt and establish Al-Qahirah, or Cairo, the modern-day capital of Egypt.

 642 AD
- Egypt is invaded by Arabs and becomes part of the Islamic Empire.

GLOSSARY

Here are some words you might come across when you're reading about ancient Egypt.

AFTERLIFE
The place ancient Egyptians believed they would go after they had died.

ANKH
The part of a person's soul that would live on in the Afterlife.

AMULET
A lucky charm worn like jewellery or placed between the bandages on a mummy.

THE BOOK OF THE DEAD
A book of spells and hymns that were thought to help the dead through the Afterlife. It was written on papyrus and placed in the burial chamber of the dead person.

BURIAL CHAMBER
The room in a tomb (or pyramid) where a mummy was placed. It was filled with objects that would be needed in the Afterlife.

CANOPIC JARS
Decorated jars containing a dead person's internal organs were stored.

CARTOUCHE
An oblong shape that symbolized eternity. Pharaohs believed that their names would live on for ever if they were written inside cartouches.

CASING STONES
The top or outer layer of a pyramid, mostly made from polished limestone.

CROOK
A gold-plated staff or shepherd's crook was carried by the pharaoh as a symbol of his duty to protect his people.

DEATH MASK
A highly decorated mask placed on a mummy to guard it on its journey to the Afterlife.

EMBALMING
Part of the process of mummification.

FLAIL
A gold, whip-like object carried by the pharaoh as a symbol of his power to punish enemies.

FUNERARY BARGE
A boat that carried a mummy to its burial place.

GREAT PYRAMID OF KHUFU
The largest of the pyramids at Giza, made for the pharaoh Khufu. It was the world's tallest building for more than 3,800 years.

HEB SED
A festival held to celebrate the rule of the pharaoh.

HIERATIC
A simplified form of hieroglyphics which was much quicker to write.

HIEROGLYPHICS
A form of Egyptian writing, using signs that resemble pictures. Hieroglyphics were complicated to write so they were used only for inscriptions on tombs and for other official or ceremonial purposes.

INUNDATION
The annual flooding of the Nile.

KA
The part of a person's soul that needed food and drink to survive. On death, it was thought to leave the body.

LOWER EGYPT
The northern area of Egypt.

MASTABA
A rectangular, flat-topped tomb made from mud-bricks and stone. Mastabas were used for high-ranking people (but not royalty – they were buried in pyramids).

MORTUARY TEMPLE
A temple built alongside a pyramid where priests made offerings to the spirits of the dead.

MUMMIFICATION
The complex process of preparing and preserving a dead body.

MUMMY
A body that has been embalmed and then wrapped in cloth strips or bandages.

NATRON
A natural salt which was used to dry out bodies during mummification.

NEMES CLOTH
A striped headdress worn by the pharaoh as a symbol of his royalty.

NILE DELTA
The place where the River Nile flows into the Mediterranean Sea. The land was extremely fertile so very good for farming.

NOMARCH
A person who governed a province, or area, of ancient Egypt on behalf of the pharaoh.

NUBIA
A region to the south of Egypt.

OBELISK
A tall stone pillar with a small pyramid at its top. Obelisks were placed at temple entrances.

OPENING OF THE MOUTH
A funeral ceremony where a priest touched the hands, feet, eyes, ears, nose and lips of the mummy with a special tool called an adze, so that the dead person could eat and drink again in the afterlife.

PAPYRUS
A reed that grows along riverbanks. It is used to make many things from boats to a form of writing paper.

PSCHENT
A double crown worn by the pharaoh.

RESIN
A sticky substance made from tree sap, used for embalming.

SARCOPHAGUS
The outer stone coffin into which a wooden coffin is laid.

SCARAB
A dung beetle that was a sacred symbol in ancient Egypt, representing new life and regeneration.

SCRIBE
A person trained to read and write. Government officials, priests, generals and the pharaoh could read and write, but most Egyptians did not go to school.

SHABTI
A small figure in the shape of a mummy, often placed in a tomb to act as a servant to the dead person in the Afterlife.

SHADUF
A device for lifting water from the river to water the fields close by.

SPHINX
A statue in the shape of a lion with a human head. The most famous example is the Great Sphinx at Giza.

UPPER EGYPT
The southern part of Egypt.

VALLEY OF THE KINGS
A valley near Thebes where pharaohs were buried in underground tombs.

VALLEY TEMPLE
A temple on the River Nile where the Opening of the Mouth ceremony may have been performed. The mummy arrived here on a funerary barge.

VIZIER
The person responsible for the day-to-day running of Egypt. Viziers collected taxes and administered justice on behalf of the pharaoh.